Mrs. Alice,

You are an amazing ...
thank you for bringing all
of us together

Joe B.

Fearless WOMAN

Born to Give Thanks

J'Anmetra "Jo-Jo" Waddell

Fearless Woman:
Born to Give Thanks

ISBN 13: 978-1514638927
ISBN 10: 1514638924
Library of Congress Control Number: 2015944558

For information, contact:
Pearly Gates Publishing LLC
Angela R. Edwards
P.O. Box 671086
Houston, TX 77267
info@angaccadminsvcs.com

Printed in the United States of America
By *CreateSpace*

DEDICATION

I would like to dedicate *Fearless Woman* to my two daughters: Kourtney and Rosamond. To me, they are the ones who are **fearless**. To walk this journey with me without complaining with the understanding that the path I have taken is not traditional is *courageous*. They are always ready for the next, new adventure in our lives.

All praises to God for who He is! He is my Foundation, my Comfort, my Safe Place, and my Healer.

To my family; my mother, sisters and brothers and friends who listened to my endless rambling about things that they had no idea about, but always lent me a listening ear: I love you all for accepting my path in life, crazy schedule, and for your support! It can never be repaid.

To the memory of my father, Gerald Waddell, and Uncle Joe Twitty: You guys have watched over and helped guide me every step of the way. My father taught me to always stand up for myself and that if I wanted to be treated as an equal, then I better bring it as an equal. My Uncle Joe taught me to stand on the Word of God and, when in doubt, sing His praises…and the answers will come. I miss you both dearly. I know you are right here with me.

To Dr. Christopher Gee: I cannot express the level of admiration and respect I have for you. You have been a continuous support. Your words of encouragement have helped me understand my journey and that distractions will come: however, it's how you handle them that makes the difference. You have blessed my daughters and me. We are truly grateful. I am humbled and thankful to call you my friend and confidant.

ACKNOWLEDGEMENTS

To my publisher, Pearly Gates Publishing LLC, who took a chance with me and allowed me the space and freedom to tell my story – my way. Angela, you are the best publisher, editor, and friend anyone can have. Thanks for understanding my wacky since of humor and laughing at my jokes!

To my numerous family and friends: Thank you for inspiring me, encouraging me, and keeping me grounded.

I beg forgiveness of all those who have been with me over the course of my years whose names I have failed to mention.

INTRODUCTION

On August 8, 2012, I read the following scriptures. It was then I felt God speak to my spirit. I knew this would be the introduction for my book. The scriptures speak of using your story of pain to help others while giving people hope that God is a Comforter. Even in our greatest tribulations, He is our Savior.

1 Peter 3:15

> *But sanctify the Lord God in your hearts; and be ready always to give an answer to every man that asketh you a reason of the hope that is in you with meekness and fear.*

II Corinthians 1:3-7

> *Blessed be God, even the Father of our Lord Jesus Christ, the Father of mercies, and the God of all comfort; who comforteth us in all our tribulation, that we may be able to comfort them which are in any trouble, by the comfort wherewith we ourselves are comforted of God. For as the sufferings of Christ abound in us, so our consolation also abounded by Christ. And whether we be afflicted, it is for your consolation and salvation, which is effectual in the enduring of the same sufferings which we also suffer: or whether we be comforted, it is for your consolation and salvation.*

This is my story. I want to share it with you so that you can share it with someone you love who may be going through a similar situation.

In the beginning, I was too afraid to write this book. It is now 2015. It is complete. Fear has no place in my life.

~ J'Anmetra Waddell

TABLE OF CONTENTS

CHAPTER ONE

The weekend before I left my now-ex-husband, Jamal, was completely insane. It was the weekend of July 26, 2004. My youngest child was finally home from the hospital after being born six weeks premature. My oldest child was seven years old at the time. I had actually gone into labor at the birthday party of the seven-year-old, so the two of them celebrate birthdays only two days apart. This particular weekend was all-around rough. It was right before my birthday when I actually left Jamal (I will get deeper into why later in the story), but I went back to him – and for good reason.

Did I mention the word "rough"? Let me explain: That Saturday, Jamal told me we were going shopping. He felt that I had cheated him out of his mama's money and I was going to have to repay every cent of it back to him – and he had just the way for me to do so.

See, at the time, we lived near an Army base. His idea of shopping involved buying me a short skirt, high heels, and taking me to the base so that I could perform oral sex or have sex with the soldiers until he felt as if I had earned his money back. All thanks to God, something happened and the latter never took place…

CHAPTER TWO

Jamal and I had to attend a church conference, and I had made up my mind to leave him during church service. His Preacher's Steward worked for the Sheriff's department...surely he would help me. During the service, I went to the restroom with the intent to sneak and place a call to the police – except all the phones in the church were gone, and the door to Jamal's clergy office was locked. That was a major problem because the church was located in the middle of nowhere – literally – miles away from what was considered "town", which was only two stores and a restaurant. I returned back to my seat defeated to listen to the rest of his sermon.

When the first service ended, we went out to eat before the next service started. I remember him venomously saying to me from across the table, "I can't stand you. I hate that I have to feed a bitch like you and your bastard child. Eat the damn food. Don't make me waste my money." The baby was in the car seat and my oldest was sitting across from me during this horrid encounter. I had absolutely no appetite, but I knew if I didn't eat, it would only get worse.

After the evening service and on the return trip home, Jamal was pin-drop silent. At one point during that evening, we were watching television in the den. He became enraged because I wasn't talking back to him. He demanded that we head upstairs to bed. As we prepared to settle down for the night, he sent my oldest child downstairs and told her, "You're not good enough to sleep upstairs with us."

As we entered the room, I recalled the bed being centered between two windows. The all-white, four-door closet was at the opposite end of the room. I remember his exact words when we entered the room: "We can either do this the soft way or the easy way." He then proceeded to tie my hands together and violently push me down across the bed. When I fell, I was facing my three-month-old daughter who was still nestled in her car seat on the floor.

He told me I better not scream. He went on to say I had married him just for his money and that I constantly made fun of him because he was fat. Because of those things, he was going to purposely hurt me – and he did. He raped and sodomized me. I just laid there and stared into my daughter's eyes while praying she would never in her life remember the moment or go through anything like this.

CHAPTER THREE

When Jamal "finished his business" with me, he untied me. I asked to go to the bathroom to clean myself up. He denied my request. What he **did** do was place a call to a family counselor. He told her I just had a mental breakdown and that he needed to have me committed to a mental hospital for my and my children's safety. Since it was the weekend, she informed him there was nothing she could do and that he would have to wait until Monday morning. Finally, he let me take my shower…and change the sheets.

As I remade the bed, I looked out the window in wonder: *If I jump, will I die? Will I survive at least enough to run and get help for my children and me? I can't just throw them out of the window. To boot, my oldest was still downstairs. What would happen to her in my absence?*

Jamal had severe sleep apnea. Unless he took his medicine, he could force himself to stay away all night long. Finally, he popped four of his pills and went into a deep sleep.

CHAPTER FOUR

The phone rang at 7:15 a.m. on July 26th. On the other end was a previous church member. She and I had been pregnant at the same time. The first time I left Jamal, I told her what happened and ended up staying at her house for a while. On this particular morning, when she called and I told her what happened, she said if I didn't leave him immediately, she was going to call 911 herself and that she wasn't hanging up the phone until I left.

By this time, I had made my way downstairs because I didn't want to wake him up. I paced the den back and forth while explaining to my friend I couldn't do it: I believed him when he said if I ever left him, he would hunt me down and kill the kids – along with my entire family. My friend was persistent. She was done hearing my excuses.

While I still had her on the phone and with as much courage as I could muster up, I quickly changed into jeans and a t-shirt and quietly told my daughter to grab one of her favorite toys. I then went upstairs, grabbed my baby (who was still asleep in her car seat), the diaper bag (with three diapers inside), a can of baby milk, and two bottles. I stood at my front door for exactly 30 minutes crying. I knew once I opened that door, the alarm would loudly announce "Door open". Finally, I agreed to leave.

In a frantic rush, I told my oldest child to take off running to the car as fast as she could as **soon** as I opened the door. I vaguely recall opening the door, but I clearly recall I didn't shut it. Together, my daughter and I ran across the yard to my red Dodge Neon. I opened the car door, hurried my oldest into the backseat, threw the baby and diaper bag in right behind her, and took off – all the while telling my daughter to hold on tight to the baby. I peeled out of there as fast as the little Neon engine would allow.

CHAPTER FIVE

I only made it about a mile before a State Trooper pulled me over. The car had no insurance, no registration, and no tags. It held only $3.00 worth of gas at a time and the front wheel constantly fell off – yet there I was, speeding through downtown in a panic. I exited the car and was hysterical. I told the trooper my abusive husband was likely hot on my trail and was going to kill my children and me. I begged the trooper to please let me go. He apologized, told me to be careful, and off my children and I went again.

That $3.00 worth of gas allowed me to travel over 80 miles to the next town. I finally stopped at a rest stop and used the change in my purse to use a pay phone to call my friend to inform her I did it: I had left him. She told me to come right over. I was far too petrified to stay with her because I knew her house would be his first stop. I ended up calling a former co-worker who allowed my children and me to stay for about a week.

During that time, I didn't eat or sleep. Most of all, I had no idea what to do with my baby. You see, I wasn't allowed to touch her because Jamal told me he was going to find himself another wife to be her mother – and he didn't want our baby girl attached to me. A majority of the time, he would bathe and change her. When I was allowed to do so, I had to do it in front of him. As such, when she cried, I had no idea how to comfort her – or anything else for that matter. As it pertained to my oldest daughter, I wasn't allowed to talk to or touch her either. Jamal said she wasn't good enough for that.

Maybe I should start at the beginning...

CHAPTER SIX

I was 24 years old when I met the pastor of my home church. My mother had invited me to come listen to a new, dynamic pastor who was taking our small community by storm. After a couple of Sundays, my mother introduced me to the pastor and told him about my work both in the community and with nonprofits. From there, we scheduled a meeting where we met with other church members about his plan to start a nonprofit for the church. This man had ideas that were going to change our small town in ways we couldn't begin to imagine.

Let me give you some background on my church. Picture a total of 30 active members – and that's exaggerating – with 20 of them being single women over the age of 50. Needless to say, all eyes were on the single pastor.

The pastor's name was Jamal. Frequently, before each service, he would be sure to mention that if he called any female member of the church, it wasn't because he was interested in her – it was strictly about handling church business.

Rev. Jamal was a well-dressed man. Everything matched: from the suit and tie, jewelry, and hat all the way down to his shoes. He had a distinguished voice. We always walked away from his sermons knowing a little bit more than we did before. He was immaculate about his speech and singing – and prided himself on his sobriety!

After a couple of meetings, Jamal and I began to talk more – one-on-one. We found we had a lot in common. The phone calls increased and there always seemed to be a reason for me to stay after service or meeting to "go over extra business".

Eventually, Rev. Jamal asked me out on a date: dinner and a movie. I recall it was during the month of July. We went to see *Scorpion King* in a neighboring state. I was very nervous the entire time. I thought other church members would find out about our tryst. I watched every car going and coming to make sure I didn't see anyone I knew. During our dinner, I kept a watchful eye on the door as well as the faces around us to make sure we weren't being watched.

CHAPTER SEVEN

The dates with Rev. Jamal became more frequent. He would come to visit me after my oldest daughter fell asleep, and we would read poetry together. We would meet for lunch every day and talk. We found ourselves talking on the phone for hours at a time. We were very careful to choose places away from where others would see us together.

On one particular excursion, we drove an hour away to a local mall to do some shopping. While there, I thought I noticed someone I knew. As I got closer, I realized it was my aunt who, just six months before, had suffered a brain aneurysm. She was paralyzed on her left side and walking with a cane, yet there she was: walking through the mall with her son. He lived in Texas but was home visiting for the weekend. Of all the people to run in to – and an hour away from home, no less!

I already knew that before we could make it back to our hometown, my aunt was going to use a pay phone to call every single solitary church member to tell them she had seen us at the mall. Of course Jamal thought I was joking – but when we returned, we both had messages on our machines telling us my aunt saw us at the mall together.

During our brief dating period, Rev. Jamal was the perfect, complete, and romantic gentleman. One time when I visited his home, there were at least 300 candles burning all over the place. We spent the night talking and continuing to get to know one another better. I felt as if I had found a match – although a slightly older version of myself.

CHAPTER EIGHT

Our relationship progressed quickly. He soon announced to the church that we were dating. My marriage proposal was "different". We were sitting in the car outside of the mall I mentioned previously. He turned to me and simply said, "We might as well get married!" I said, "Sure! Okay." In September of 2002, we were married at the courthouse. Our witnesses were people who just so happened to walk out the courtroom door; a young black man and white girl. I remember feeling so sick during the ceremony, I thought I was going to vomit all over the place.

My family, friends, and church family were furious. You see, Jamal had started to monopolize my time. He started to say little things that, at first, were so sweet, cute, and thoughtful – like:

'The library was too far', so I should just read his books.

'My family was too demanding of my time', so I should just spend my time with him.

Eventually, he had taken claim to everything about my life – from dropping off and picking me up from work, to coming home for lunch every day. Every single weekend was spent together. My oldest daughter was five years old at the time, and I have to admit: she hated him. She begged me not to marry him and told me once that she thought he was a mean, old man. Oh, how I wished I had listened to my child – I mean *really* heard her.

CHAPTER NINE

When I first told my family Jamal and I were getting married, they lost their minds! Some threatened to burn the church down to the ground. Some called our Presiding Elder. With the exception of **three members**, *everyone* else stopped coming to church. If they saw me on the street, they wouldn't speak or even look in my direction. They talked about me so bad, I only wanted to go to work and return home to Jamal.

I was mentally hurt and drained. Those who did the damage were women and men who taught me everything I knew about being a Christian and what it meant to be a woman. I didn't understand any of it. My family members contacted the governing board of our denomination in a frantic attempt to try to stop our marriage. My mother and sister threatened to burn the church down if we had a ceremony there and eventually, before we moved, my family had stopped talking to me altogether.

CHAPTER TEN

The first time Jamal put his hands on me was when I was home for lunch from the doctor's office. He cornered me and asked where I had been. He then grabbed me by my neck and pushed me into his desk chair. I remember thinking in a fog: **What is going on here?** He actually struck me twice in a row. I recall crying and screaming at him – and he, of course, apologized and said he didn't know what had come over him.

By December of the same year, Jamal decided we needed to move. His favorite place was Raleigh, North Carolina. Christmas Eve, we packed up our apartment and I remember thinking, "Why is it raining tonight of all nights?" I remember wanting to cry because only my stepfather showed up to say good-bye. My mother nor anyone else from my family contacted me, either. It ended up being the last time I had the opportunity to see any of them for two years.

CHAPTER ELEVEN

Often, Rev. Jamal made it a point to announce to the church that he was going to be a quarter of a million dollars richer in a couple of months. *Let me just mention here that his mother had passed away and left him the money in her life insurance policy. That will be an extremely important point later on in this story.* It was with that money that we found a place to live, put my daughter in school, and helped me find a job. Of course, every weekend we continued to drive 3 ½ hours back "home" so he could conduct Sunday service.

CHAPTER TWELVE

I honestly can't say I recall the first time Jamal hit me once we moved to Raleigh; I just know it seemed to be an everyday kind of thing. Either I said or did something that made him fly into a rage for hours at a time. One thing he loved to do was send my daughter to her room. He would then spend the entire day spewing out the following words – and to this day, I can still hear them clearly in my head and repeat them word-for-word:

- You're ugly.

- You're stupid.

- You will never be anything.

- You're a nobody.

- I don't know who told you you're pretty; you're fat.

- You had better be glad I married you; no one else wants you but me.

- Your family doesn't love you; they don't care anything about you.
- You tricked me into marrying you; you lied to me.
- You only wanted my money.
- You made me waste my mama's money on you and your bastard child.

His tirade would last easily six to eight hours – daily. He would do the majority of the talking and then ask questions like "What do you have to say for yourself?" or "How are you going to fix this relationship?" Sometimes, however, I was given a pass – if I was "a good girl" – and he wouldn't say anything else.

It was during those times that I developed other ways to occupy my mind so that I wouldn't go insane. I would count the tiles in the ceiling, multiply by odd numbers, or find the smallest piece of lint on my red sweater to roll under my fingernails – just to see how long I could hold it without dropping it. *I loved that red sweater. It belonged to one of my former college classmates. The sweater was too big and had two large pockets on the side, but it became my security blanket.*

It's amazing the things you remember or concentrate on when you are overwhelmed.

CHAPTER THIRTEEN

Jamal decided we needed to have a child because he had given up his parental rights to his daughter. He wanted the chance to be a father again. My first pregnancy by him ended in a miscarriage. One night, during an argument, he pulled me off the bed and I fell to the floor – hard. I remember reaching underneath the bed to grab a shoe to hit him with. Of course **that** didn't end well.

A couple of days later while I was at work, my stomach started to ache. By the middle of the day, I was bleeding profusely and unable to leave the bathroom. I tried calling Jamal, but he didn't answer his phone. I called the YMCA because his daily routine included going there from 10:00 a.m. to 3:00 p.m. to work out, play basketball, and network. After a while, I finally contacted another minister friend of ours. The wife was at work, but her husband was available to come pick me up. By the time the man arrived, Jamal had returned my call and said he was on his way.

On the way to the hospital, Jamal argued and argued with me about his wife calling on another man to do his job. He didn't care how bad I was hurting or the least bit concerned about what was going on with my body. I was to never again call another man for help. When we reached the hospital, I had completely miscarried the baby. Jamal was devastated and said it was completely my fault. Had I not been a whore my entire life, I could have carried our child. I spent a few days at home before I had to return to work. His philosophy was this: It was my job to work while it was his job to focus on ministry.

CHAPTER FOURTEEN

Often, when we fell behind on the rent, Jamal would leave it up to me to find the money to pay the bills. One month, the rent was so late, we received an eviction notice. His routine didn't suffer. He got up and went to the gym. His instructions before leaving were, "Find the money for the rent...or else." I went to the courthouse and arranged with an attorney to pay the rent. I spent the remainder of the day begging and pleading for money from support agencies.

I clearly recall being on the floor that day on bended knee, crying out to and pleading with God to *please* give me the money to pay the rent and bills.

CHAPTER FIFTEEN

I always loved the times I would wake up early. Jamal would still be asleep, and I could go into my oldest daughter's room to hug, kiss, and get her ready for school. It was our special quiet time. The only 'normal' thing I did was have prayer with another minister's wife every morning at 6:00 a.m. sharp. Occasionally, I would also watch a few minutes of whatever I wanted to on television – or perhaps read a book I had acquired from work. It was during those few moments in the morning that I was *free*. In the reverse, if Jamal was up, the day usually started with an argument – depending on "which side of the bed" he woke up on. Often, he would decide whether or not I went to work. If we had an argument the night before, I couldn't **WAIT** to get to work!

One time, my car broke down and I had no way to get to work. I had made friends with a woman at work who lived one street over from me who offered me a ride to and from work. For quite a while, I heavily depended on her as my transport – unless Jamal decided differently. I had no money to give her for gas, and Jamal didn't give me any to offer her. My weekly allowance was usually only $3.00 to $6.00 a week…from **MY** paycheck. I'm sure she felt used by me.

I used to call her on some mornings and tell her to not pick me up. Jamal would them tell me to find my own way to work. I couldn't drive his car and I had no money to call a cab – but I BETTER get to work because I had to pay the bills. Mind you, my job was over 15 miles away. However, if I stayed at home and wasn't being paid to do so, Jamal was going to beat me for missing out on money to be made.

CHAPTER SIXTEEN

One day, I was almost out the door heading to work. Jamal and I had been arguing most of the night and all of the morning. I was sure I could make it out the door free from the onslaught of verbal abuse… Actually, I did make it completely out the door – then he flung the door open and jerked me back inside by my jacket. That jerking action literally lifted me out of my shoes! I remember looking over at my next door neighbor who was standing on her front porch smoking a cigarette. She just looked at me and then turned away as he pulled me all the way in and slammed the door shut. That was how my day began.

I became an expert storyteller (a.k.a. liar). At work, I wore heavy makeup to cover the bruises or avoided eye contact. However, work was the only place I was free to be me. I was able to laugh, make friends, and pretend that everything was okay. Years later, I contacted some of those previous co-workers. What they told me shocked me. The gist was that they said they were afraid to tell me just how bad I looked. They said I looked like death was chasing me and that they feared for my life. Admittedly, they didn't know how to help me.

CHAPTER SEVENTEEN

My life had become so heavily controlled by Jamal that I often wondered if my thoughts were my own.

One morning, he walked in on me while I was using the bathroom. I had my hand under my leg as I was sitting on the toilet. He asked me why I used the bathroom that way, and I told him I hated sitting on a cold seat. As well, as a girl, I was taught to not sit directly on the toilet. He said that was the craziest thing he had ever heard and from that point on, I was to use the bathroom the way he instructed me to – which required me sitting fully on the seat. In addition, I had to leave the door open so he could make sure I did it exactly the way he commanded.

From that point forward, if I was home, he controlled when I could use the bathroom and when I ate. There were times when I ate once a day and went to the bathroom once a day. My "me-time" became the shower. I would stay in there as long as I could before he started to yell. I would sometimes stand in the bathroom with the shower running but not bathing. I would be in a daze staring out the window into our backyard while chanting over and over again: "I know I'm not crazy. I know I'm not crazy. I'm *not* crazy."

CHAPTER EIGHTEEN

In the beginning of our relationship, Jamal would try to win over my daughter. He was the sweetest thing with her. Eventually, he began to mention little things like: "She doesn't listen very well" or he would ask her "Do you hear your mother talking to you? Please obey." At first, I thought, *"Great! I have someone to help me raise my daughter! We are going to be a great family!"* It didn't take long for all of that to change.

When we moved to Raleigh, he was constantly telling her she was a bad little girl and that she wasn't worthy enough to spend time with us because she was acting up in school, not paying attention, and a laundry list of other things. Somehow, he always found something she was doing wrong. During our first year of marriage, she spent most of each day in her bedroom.

Watching him deal with her in that way was one of the most depressing things. At the same time, it was also something I was *grateful* for: She was away from danger. During the course of our marriage, Jamal was convinced he was a better parent than her father. He actually called her father and requested that he sign over his parental rights so that he could adopt my daughter. Thankfully, that didn't happen.

CHAPTER NINETEEN

He wanted her to be seen and not heard. He was convinced she was a terrible child. Almost immediately, she was confined to her room – all day long. When she came home from school, she had to go straight to her room. She was permitted to come out for dinner and to bathe, but she was not allowed to watch television or spend any time with us – unless he was in a good mood. This went on for the entirety of the two years we were married. I was ashamed. At the same time, I knew it was the only thing that was keeping her safe and kept her from getting hurt.

The one time I talked to my mother during our two-year marriage was when Jamal called her and told her to come pick up my daughter because she had gotten into trouble at school. My mother arrived to pick her up, but before she did, Jamal made me leave the house. I had a black eye that no amount of makeup could cover, and he didn't want her to see me or try to make me leave him. I didn't have an opportunity to see my daughter leave with my mother.

He called me after they left and told me I could return. Don't ask me why I didn't keep on driving or reach out for help. Abusers have control over your life long before they ever hit you. They have control over your mind, thoughts, and actions – and you trust and believe they will carry out any threats.

When I returned home, Jamal was sitting on the couch crying. Behind him was a tall candle holder. He removed the candle and started violently stabbing it into the pointy pick of the holder. As he was doing the stabbing, he said to me, "You made me send that child away. How could you, as a mother, make me do that? What kind of mother are you?" He kept stabbing the candle and crying. I walked out the back door thinking, "He is going to kill me tonight while my daughter is gone."

Eventually, I went back inside. When I did, he calmly said, "Get the computer, reserve a car, and go pick up our daughter." I did just that then called my mother and told her I was on my way to pick her up. I made the 3 ½ hour trip alone. Jamal's instructions were clear: I was to pick her up and come right back.

When I arrived at my mother's house, it was full of everyone I knew. I also knew it was going to be beyond difficult. The entire time I was there, I spent it trying to convince them – and me – that everything was perfect. I was fine, my marriage was fine, and all was well with the world. I simply wanted my daughter. I wouldn't let anyone hug me too close because I didn't want the extra makeup I had put on to rub off on their shirts, which would have caused them to ask more questions. I returned home to Jamal and things went back to my 'normal'.

CHAPTER TWENTY

I became a professional makeup artist from the many instances of covering up black eyes and bruises around my neck and on my face. I wore sunglasses year around – even in the winter months when it grew dark before it was time to pick up my daughter. The daycare providers never asked me about what they saw, but I could still see the look of pity on their faces – even with the sunglasses on. A few of them did ask, "Why the sunglasses?" I would reply with some off-hand answer, but none of them reached out to me to ask if I was okay.

Remember my red Dodge Neon? The one with the broken gas tank that would hold only $3.00 worth of gas at a time? The one with the wobbly front wheel that had only one stud holding it in place? One day, when picking my oldest daughter up from daycare, the teacher was so worried I was going to wreck on the way home, she followed me all the way. When we arrived, she got out of her car crying because she thought my wheel was going to fall off during the trip home and that I was going to die. Jamal was well aware of the situation. Some mornings, I was allowed to take his car to work. Most mornings, I wasn't.

CHAPTER TWENTY-ONE

We were assigned a new church in the Raleigh area, so that eliminated our 3 ½ hour drive every Sunday morning back 'home'. The church had 10 members – all from the same family starting with the grandparents on down. Their church had recently burned down and they had no meeting place to hold services. Eventually, a local church let us use their sanctuary after their service on Sunday. That meant we didn't start service until 1:00 p.m. The salary from this church didn't help the stress at home. It was only $75.00 – every two weeks.

One of the funniest things happened during service one Sunday. Right in the middle of the sermon, the grandmother stood up and said, "Pastor, I would really love for my son to sing me my favorite song." The son jumped up and sang the song! I dare not laugh out loud, of course. After all, who challenged the great pastor?

I became close friends with one of the female members of the church. We soon found out we were pregnant at the same time. Our daughters were born two months apart and, in the end, she was the one to help save my life.

My sister came to visit me once while we were at this church. As I think back on it now, I can only imagine how ridiculous I must have looked and acted. I remember driving to service that Sunday morning and telling my sister, "You have to love your man. I love mine." All the while, I was lovingly rubbing Jamal's shoulder and head. When we stopped at a store for him to get a drink, I stopped talking. It was as if I had never even opened my mouth to say those things. When he returned, however, I went right back to acting happy and loving.

CHAPTER TWENTY-TWO

We were assigned a new church. It was bigger and had at least 40 members. It was located in a small, rural town in eastern North Carolina. The churchyard was part of a train track. The women there were so sweet. It was there I met the mother of a young woman I would later become friends with. This church paid a little more than the last. It helped, but on the other hand, not *really*.

The women of this church absolutely adored their new pastor and always provided Sunday dinner or fulfilled whatever needs he had. They treated me with nothing but respect – although it was rather obvious I was younger than he and was new at being a "pastor's wife". As we approached the end of Jamal's tenure there, the women would always bring me to the altar every Sunday morning to pray for me. I always thought it was the sweetest thing. After all, who needed prayer more than me?

It wasn't until later that Jamal told me they were only praying for me because he had told them I had mental and emotional problems – and that he was trying to love me through my pains. So, in actuality, they were praying for **his** strength and for **me** to recognize what a great husband I had.

CHAPTER TWENTY-THREE

In public, Jamal was an amazing man! Every Sunday morning – or whenever he had an occasion to speak in front of a congregation – I would introduce him. When he got up to speak, his first words always included, "…and to my lovely and beautiful wife, J'Anmetra, without whom I am absolutely nothing." Of course, I would smile and say, "Thank you." The women around me ate it up! They would pat me on the shoulder and tell me how beautiful of a husband I have – one who loves me so much. I would sometimes hear other preachers' wives say, "I wish my husband would do that."

When people saw me on any given day – especially at a church event – my 3-karat wedding ring with matching bracelet and earrings were sparkling. My hair and makeup were always done and, when it was cold, my full-length fur coat with matching hat were on point! I wore the atypical big hats with the matching outfits. I knew all the right things to say. I taught Sunday school and Bible Study. I presented to the world the **best** preacher's wife possible.

Inside, I wanted someone to stop me – to stop it all – but it seemed as if it would never *ever* end...

CHAPTER TWENTY-FOUR

Let me ask you this: Have you ever been driving and looked at the people in the car next to you while wondering what was going on in their world? I did. When Jamal and I traveled, it was often in dead silence. *Sometimes* the music was on. Oftentimes, there was nothing either of us had to say. I would talk to myself a lot during long rides. I would tell myself, "Okay, JoJo. Say something now... Okay, how about NOW? Well? What are you waiting for? Say something! Anything! SAY SOMETHING!" I remained speechless. I could never find the inner-strength to open my mouth to say a word. I would just stare out the window and watch the world go by. I often wondered if people could tell I was miserable and was likely going to die in this relationship. I didn't know when, but I knew I was going to die by Jamal's hands. *Would they tell my parents I loved them? What about my favorite uncle Joe? What would my daughter think of me? Would Jamal tell her I killed myself?*

Once I discovered I was pregnant again, we made friends with some of the younger members of the church. There were two couples – both with children – and we invited them over for dinner often. We had great conversations about how we were going to change the culture of the church and how things were going to be different. Together, we worked to start a nonprofit. We spent many weekends working closely together. Those days were filled with lots of laughter and comradery.

CHAPTER TWENTY-FIVE

Being pregnant didn't stop the abuse; it came in other forms such as mental and emotional abuse.

One night, I was in the living room alone – moments that were very rare. *I cannot recall a time I was ever truly alone – other than at 6:00 a.m. for prayer.* Anyway, on this particular night, I was watching TV and he was down the hall in the bedroom. I wanted some pizza, so I headed into the kitchen to warm up a slice. The floor had been mopped in the kitchen, but by the time I made it in there, it was mostly dry. There was a small puddle…nothing of major concern. I heated up my slice, returned to the living room, and enjoyed eating my piece of pizza – until Jamal came into the living room.

When asked what I was eating, I told him, "Pizza." He asked, "From the kitchen?" I responded, "Yes." Here's where it went downhill… He said, "You walked on the wet floor to get it?" I explained, "No. The floor is not wet. There are maybe two wet spots on the floor. I walked around them." *Note here, reader: The kitchen was a galley style and extremely small. At best, two people standing side-by-side could fit – but no more than two.* Jamal made me get up just so he could show me the water on the floor. *Sigh*

When I sat back down, I took another bite of pizza and started to chew. Suddenly, he grabbed my cheeks and pinched them so hard I thought my jawbone was going to break. He told me in that moment I better **never** walk on a wet floor again. The following morning, there was no amount of makeup that could cover the pink spots left on my cheeks. I was all out of creative stories, too. No one asked, so I had nothing to explain.

CHAPTER TWENTY-SIX

My pregnancy was not an easy one. I was so stressed out, it was unreal. One visit to the doctor revealed I didn't have enough amniotic fluid to support the baby. The doctor called us in and gave us the news. Jamal's questions shocked the doctor into silence at first. He asked, "Is the baby going to have Down Syndrome? Are there going to be other problems?" I remember the doctor's puzzled look as he looked from me to him a couple of times. The doctor's response broke the uncomfortable silence. He said, "Sir, what does that have to do with you having a baby? What do you want to do? It's too late to terminate the pregnancy. The only thing we can do now is work towards having a healthy baby."

The date was March 2004. From that day on, I was on complete bedrest.

I thought I was going to lose my mind!

CHAPTER TWENTY-SEVEN

One day during my pregnancy, I was feeling very sick and kept vomiting. I had the flu. I told Jamal I needed to go to the hospital. He helped me get dressed and to the car. He drove around town with no particular destination in mind – although I just knew eventually we would end up at the hospital. During the excursion, I fell asleep. When I woke up, we were back home. He said, "You don't need a doctor. You just need to take this and you will feel better." The 'this' was a bottle of wine. *You see, he was a recovering alcoholic. It is that story he takes great pride in: his sobriety.* I had never consumed alcohol and wasn't about to start. Nonetheless, he poured a glass for me and set it by the bed. I didn't drink it. That, of course, enraged him.

To this day, I have no idea what happened to that bottle of wine.

He **said** he poured it out.

CHAPTER TWENTY-EIGHT

In April 2004, we threw a party for my oldest daughter's birthday. Two couples from church were in attendance. Both had children my daughter's age. Right before we started to sing 'Happy Birthday', my insides began to cramp. I went to the bedroom to lie down for a few minutes. Before too long, I insisted that my doctor be called. The doctor told us to meet him at the hospital immediately because I was in labor.

Everyone in attendance at the party followed us to the hospital – a 30-minute trip to the next city over. Once I arrived, the doctor examined me and informed me I was in active labor. *Wait. What? My due date wasn't until June!*

All the while, my blood pressure was sky-rocketing. I was unable to hear on my left side and I had lost my vision in my left eye. The doctor came in and said, "We are flying you to Bowman Gray Hospital. We can't handle your or your baby here." I was petrified! I was not flying anywhere! Eventually, they were able to bump a mother from Duke University Hospital and I was admitted there.

.   Once I arrived at Duke, my blood pressure was worse. They were afraid I was going to have a heart attack. I was placed on every medication available in a frantic attempt to regulate the problem. Did I fail to mention I was now on day two of active labor and rising blood pressure? The situation was critical. It was either the baby or me. The doctors were unsure whether they could save both of us. Eventually, they decided to induce my labor, get the baby out quickly, and then work on saving my life.

The final attempt to induce labor was made and the doctor told me he would see me in a couple of hours. Roughly 40 minutes later, I reached down and could feel the baby's head. The staff immediately came in and rolled me down to the delivery room. My daughter was born weighing one pound. I saw her when they held her tiny body in the air for a quick second. I was so drugged up from the medications, I really don't remember much more than that.

CHAPTER TWENTY-NINE

I woke up a few hours later in my room thinking I was still in labor – except it was much, much worse than that. I told Jamal to call the nurse. When she arrived, she started yelling for the doctor. She grabbed a stool, pulled it up to my bedside, and reached in between my legs trying to stop the bleeding. All the while, she was screaming for the doctor. I mustered up the strength to turn my head to look down at her feet – and they were covered with my blood. I passed out.

When I came to, the same nurse was standing over me. The hallways lights were whizzing by. The doctors and nurses were yelling back and forth to one another. I could hear the panic in their voices. I remember one saying, "She's not going to make it through this while awake." One doctor called my name and told me to count to two. His voice was the last one I heard. When I woke up, I was gagging on the line that was coming out of my throat. The nurse kept rubbing my back telling me 'it was okay'. I couldn't talk. My throat hurt. My body hurt. I couldn't hear clearly. The sight in my left eye was gone. "It's okay." Really?

If only she knew…

CHAPTER THIRTY

I honestly cannot recall when I made it back to my room. When I awoke, there was Jamal. He was on the phone with my mother. He told her I had a baby; no, she couldn't see the child; and no, she couldn't talk to me. I fell back to sleep. When I woke up again, he was so attentive. I knew it was too good to be true. I realized it was an act for the nurses in the room. As soon as they left, he came to my bedside and said, "I wish you had died, bitch, so you wouldn't have to raise my child and save me the trouble." *His words verbatim. Nothing was left out.* I just looked at him and fell back asleep.

I woke up to yelling, cussing, and screaming. I didn't know where I was. I heard my mother's and Jamal's voices. Apparently, he had called security and told them my mother, sister, and aunt were not allowed in the room to see me and they were not allowed to see the baby. He said he wanted them removed from the hospital. Of course, my family (true to form) threatened to burn the hospital down! The three of them left without ever visiting me or seeing the baby. My mother called the room later. All I could do was cry and ask her to just let me rest.

The nurse arrived after the confrontation and asked if I was okay. I responded, "Of course!" For some reason, she obviously didn't believe me. She would not leave the situation alone – although I never said a word to her about it.

I was finally able to see my daughter. It had to have been three or four days after her birth. She was so tiny and had a lot of tubes running in and out of her. I couldn't touch or hold her. I could barely walk, see, or hear. I thought, *"If I die now, at least she would make it."*

CHAPTER THIRTY-ONE

I was advised I needed a blood transfusion because of the large amount of blood loss from having the baby and during surgery. I decided against it. The doctor told me that without it, I would be on bedrest for another two months. I lost so much blood, I needed rest. I needed to allow my body to heal.

Five days after my daughter's birth, I was released to go home. She had to stay. It was so hard to leave her behind, but I had no choice. Soon, she was transferred to a local hospital closer to home. The week before she was scheduled to come home, Jamal and I needed to get the house ready for her arrival. 'Getting ready' included putting the crib together. The night before we had to go to the hospital to bring our baby home, we were doing just that: putting the crib together. Jamal decided he would rather watch and not help – at all. He found pleasure in watching me struggle to piece it together. In the end, he helped and I was allowed to go to bed.

I was supposed to spend the day and night at the hospital so I could get used to my baby. However, I arrived late because Jamal didn't feel the need for me to spend that much time with her. He hated that I breast fed her. I received a black eye for allowing the nurse to force my baby to take my breast so that she could learn to eat.

Even with my screaming baby in the room, in that hospital bed was the best sleep I had in a long time.

CHAPTER THIRTY-TWO

Our baby stayed in the hospital for 31 days after her birth. When we went to visit her, the nurses would try to get her to breast feed. That enraged Jamal. On the way home, he would scream at me for allowing the nurse to try to force the baby to take my nipple. He said, "If she wanted it, she would take it."

He didn't care that breast milk was what was best for her – especially after being born premature. After a couple of unsuccessful tries, I was instructed to tell the nurse we would be using the bottle. That allowed him to feed her while not allowing for me to get attached to her.

After all, I wouldn't be around long enough for any of that to matter.

My life **was** on the line…daily. It is no longer that way.

CHAPTER THIRTY-THREE

After our daughter came home from the hospital, it was time for me to return to the workforce – despite the doctor's order for me to remain on bedrest for two months. My friend (the one who was pregnant the same time as me) had an opening in her office, and I started working there immediately.

On day two of working at my new job, my husband called and said, "I'm on my way to pick you up." I was standing out front of the building when I saw his car pull up. I ran back inside to grab my purse. When I returned, he was talking to one of our previous church members. We said our goodbyes and left.

As I put my seatbelt on, he asked, "What took you so long? Where were you when I pulled up?" I said, "I saw you pull up, so I went to grab my purse." He responded, "No you didn't. I didn't see you when I pulled up." When we stopped at a red light, I saw him "preparing" his hand – the one he wore a pinky ring on. Suddenly, he hit me in my throat – pinky ring and all. He asked, "Are you lying to me?" I yelled, "No!" Then he hit me in my forehead. By the time the forehead pop happened, he had pulled over behind a building. He then hit me in my chest. In an accusing tone, he screamed, "You are going to stop lying to me. I saw you looking at that man. You were not where I told you to be when I get there."

The baby was in the backseat and she started to cry. That snapped him back to reality. He drove home. When we entered the house, he sat the baby – in her car seat – on the couch. He turned to me and asked, "You think you're smart and funny, don't you?" Before I could say a word, he grabbed me by my hair and dragged me down the hallway. He threw me on the bed, climbed on top of me (all 250+ pounds of him), and started to choke me. I couldn't scream or breathe. As I looked at him – right into his eyes – they were blank. There was nothing there: no love…no hate…just nothingness. That was the last thing I saw.

When I came to and looked around, I heard heavy breathing. Jamal was leaning against the wall out of breath. He said, "You better thank God I didn't kill you." Then he walked out of the room.

My necklace was broken and my earrings had been snatched out of my ears. I continued to lay there and stared at the ceiling. When I went into the bathroom and looked in the mirror, there they were: a black eye and a red neck. I put on makeup, but there was no covering the black eye.

The time came to get my oldest daughter from daycare, but he said, "No. She can stay at school." I told him if I didn't pick her up, social services would. He said, "No problem. She's not my child anyway."

Eventually, I was allowed to go pick her up – five minutes before the daycare center closed. When I arrived, it was dark. There I was with sunglasses on – but I dare not remove them considering I was battered and bruised.

CHAPTER THIRTY-FOUR

Our family moved to a new house – one that was another hour away from "home". We rented a beautiful split-level home. To the left was the formal living room that branched off to the kitchen. The kitchen had custom granite countertops, hardwood floors, and bay windows that looked over the back yard. From the kitchen, it stepped down into the formal dining room and then continued on into the den. Also on the first floor was a bathroom and bedroom. The top floor housed two bedrooms and a bathroom.

The first time I left Jamal, it was three days before my birthday: June 26th. We had spent the day in the den having our usual conversation: me getting lectured on how stupid I was and how I was nothing but a prostitute. My oldest daughter was upstairs asleep, and the baby was in the room with us. I asked if I could be excused to go to the bathroom (*I didn't **really** have to go...I just needed a **BREAK***). In that moment, something told me to grab the car keys and *GO*.

The bathroom was Jack and Jill style. I went in one way, out another through the office, and walked right out the front door. It had to be about 10:00 p.m.! I climbed into the rental car (ours had broken down right before we moved) and started driving. I was determined to find a hospital to talk to anyone. I needed to find out whether or not I was crazy! I was thoroughly convinced I was everything I was being told.

CHAPTER THIRTY-FIVE

The first place I went to wasn't actually a hospital, so I left. Since we were fairly new to the area, I had no idea where the hospital was. I eventually found and followed the signs for our local hospital and checked myself in. When the attendant asked me what was wrong, I told him about the abuse. He made me write a statement that said I would not contact my husband to tell him where I was. I was then taken to the back to wait on someone to speak with me.

They gave me a psych evaluation and then a counselor came to talk to me. After we were done, I have to say: I had the best few hours of sleep – a few hours of peaceful rest out of two years! When I awoke, I turned my phone on. I felt so bad for leaving my children alone with Jamal. I wasn't there to protect them. I ended up telling him where I was and waited for him to come. When he arrived, the police asked me if I wanted to see him. I told them no. They told me the law states whoever has the children with them cannot be forced to give them to the other spouse. Fortunately, I was able to get my oldest daughter because she wasn't his child. However, he kept the baby.

This all happened on a Friday night.

CHAPTER THIRTY-SIX

The police took me to a women's shelter. I called my friend and asked her to come pick me up. The shelter instructed me to walk up the street to meet her so that the safety of the shelter wouldn't be jeopardized. I was so scared and nervous. When we arrived at her house, I couldn't sleep. The next day, I just **knew** he was going to find me.

Sure enough, that next day Jamal called my friend to ask if she had seen me – and to tell her he wanted his wife home. She spent about three hours on the phone with him. The entire time, I paced the floor. When she exited her room, she walked over to me, hugged me, and said, "I am so sorry. I don't know how you could sit and listen to him talk all day." Some of the things he told her frightened her. She was afraid that if I went back, he would kill me.

Later that night, there was an intervention on my behalf. My friend, her husband, and another couple (their parents were members of our church) sat me down and tried to convince me not to go back to Jamal. One of the husbands finally "kept it real". He said, "You guys might as well stop talking. She is going back, and there's nothing you can do or say about it." I didn't speak much during the intervention – although they all tried to convince me that I was going to die or that he was going to seriously hurt the children and me. I **had** to go back. There was absolutely no way I *couldn't*.

CHAPTER THIRTY-SEVEN

When I spoke to Jamal over the phone, the conversation was the same: "Please come back. I will never hit you again." This time, however, was different for me. I was feeling brave and told him, "I cannot take you hitting me anymore. It's not right." He agreed and told me, "Just come home. We will go to counseling and work it out. I will do whatever it takes to make our marriage work." After the call, the couple whose parents were my church members finally spoke up. The room fell silent. The husband said, "She's going back. There's nothing else we can say. She's going back to him." He was correct.

The following morning, I packed up my oldest child and we set off back to Fayetteville. I could not leave my baby girl down there alone with him. I didn't want her to think I left her – and I knew that would be the story told.

Live or die, I had to go back home.

CHAPTER THIRTY-EIGHT

When I returned home, Jamal was glad to see me. My oldest daughter immediately went to her room. Jamal and I headed upstairs to ours. Everything was okay – well okay as it could be. My birthday was June 29th. That day, I was treated to a nice dinner date and a nice night out on the town.

Early in July, the doorbell rang. It was social services doing a routine welfare check on the children and me. The called before they came, which gave Jamal the opportunity to have "the conversation" – the one where he said that if I told them what really happened, they would take our kids…and he added he would kill me if anything happened to his daughter. That meant I better lie and tell the worker he never hit me.

When the social worker arrived, he spoke with us together and then again separately. He told me it was a serious offense to lie on a pastor and that I should be careful of what I say. The worker also spoke to my oldest daughter. She lied, too. She was scared if she didn't, she would never see me again. The worker advised us to keep at least two weeks' worth of food in the house at all times. As he was leaving, he stated he would return in 30 days for another visit. After the worker left, Jamal told me I had done well and that if I didn't want them to take our children away, I would never tell anyone what was going on in our home.

After the visit, everything was fine for a while – until I cooked his dinner "wrong". Things went back to the way they were… That night, dinner was cubed steak with peppers and onions. When Jamal joined me in the kitchen to ask what I was making, I told him. He looked at me and said it was all wrong: He liked his steak cooked with the peppers and onions first – and then I should have added the gravy.

That opened up the floor for a discussion – well, not really a discussion but rather a rant – about how I never follow instructions, directions, or do anything right. Pan and all went into the trash. He wanted his dinner cooked again…his way.

CHAPTER THIRTY-NINE

Remember: One of the things Jamal promised me was that we would go to counseling. I found a female counselor willing to take us who was reasonably priced. During the first visit, we introduced ourselves and she talked with each of us (my oldest daughter, too) separately. It was during that first session that Jamal laid the groundwork for what would later become his foundation for the future.

The sessions were held once a week. The counselor never talked to Jamal and me separately. Jamal did most of the talking. I just sat there and stared at the wall. In my mind, however, I was **screaming**: *"Please help me! Save me! He is lying!"* – but those words never exited my mouth. When I **was** asked to speak, I knew all the right things to say: "Yes, I am lazy. Yes, I'm a horrible parent. Yes, I'm a liar. No, I don't love my husband. No, I don't cook or clean."

By the end of the first month – four sessions into 'repairing our marriage' – the counselor told me I was what they called a "functional retard". She said I was mentally-disturbed and that I needed to snap out of it because the world didn't owe me anything. *What she didn't know was that I had specific instructions on what to say and not say during those sessions.*

By the time our second month of counseling came around, I had left Jamal and came back. As we proceeded to leave the house for a counseling session, he suddenly stopped and said he didn't think we should go. When I asked why not, he said, "The last time I let you out of here, you left me, told lies on me, and had people in our business." It took a lot of coaxing to convince him that we should go and not miss the appointment. In all actuality, for me, it was just to get out of the house and see someone else. After being cooped up in a room for eight to 10 hours with Jamal listening to him rant, I was mentally exhausted. Seeing the counselor was a break – *for my mind*.

CHAPTER FORTY

Church anniversary came around, and as usual, there was arguing amongst the choir members about what to sing. After practice, I pulled the director aside and asked if they could sing Jamal's favorite song during the service. Of course she agreed and was excited to do anything to please her pastor.

When word got back to Jamal that I had asked them to sing his favorite song, we were in a hotel room. My oldest daughter was asleep on the other bed when he came over to me and asked, "Are you messing in my church's business?" I wasn't sure what he was talking about – until he said the director of the choir told him the choir was going to sing his favorite song during service on Sunday. "How did she know my favorite song?" he asked. I told him, "I told her. It was supposed to be a surprise." He slapped me so hard, I fell across the bed. He followed up the slap by saying, "Never mess in my church business again. It's mine; not yours. I don't want them to know my business like that."

CHAPTER FORTY-ONE

Jamal didn't call what he did 'cheating'. He often denied looking at pornography. When I asked him about it, he eventually stopped responding to my questions. He called the online-dating that he was doing while we were married as him "doing research for a new mother for his child". He didn't want me to raise her because, as he said, I wasn't a good mother or role model. He wanted to find someone to take my place who I could train before he killed me – so that my youngest daughter would grow up to believe 'that woman' was her mother.

CHAPTER ONE

Prelude to Transition to Freedom

THE DAY AFTER I LEFT JAMAL...

The day I left was filled with crazy things. Thank goodness my friend was thinking for me because I was on robot-mode. She had me change my address to hers so that I could receive my unemployment check. She made sure I had clothes by taking me to a local consignment shop and telling them I was going through. They gave me a $100.00 voucher for clothing. It is a humbling experience to have to buy second-hand underwear, bras, and everything. Even the small things you take for granted that are no longer at your fingertips – like a toothbrush, comb, diapers, milk, and money.

Jamal called my friend that day and asked if she had seen me and she told him no. He told her his only worry was for the children and he wanted to make sure they had everything they needed. Since the baby was premature, she needed certain milk, clothes, etc. and he was just so worried.

I went to the bank the next day to withdraw some money out of the account because my unemployment check had been deposited. When I arrived, the teller said, "Ms. Jamal, this account has been closed." I told her, "That's impossible! My unemployment check is direct-deposited into it!" She replied, "No, ma'am. It's not. Mr. Jamal closed this bank account on yesterday." He cleaned out the checking and savings accounts (not that there was much in there). I guess he wasn't worried too much about his daughter having milk and diapers...the three diapers I had taken when we left were long gone.

I had to have charges pressed against Jamal if I wanted him to stay away. My friend took me to the courthouse and I was a nervous wreck. Walking into the doors, I was shaking and could barely talk. The police promised to take care of me and they issued a warrant for his arrest. They told me I had to show back up at court two weeks later to testify. I felt the room go dark, and I wasn't sure if I was sitting or standing. My skin was both hot and cold. I didn't want to ever see him again. How was I going to stand in front of and testify against him?

My story doesn't end there.

What will happen next?

Look for the exciting conclusion

– *Transition to Freedom* –

coming January 2016!

The *Fearless Woman* workbook and journal will be released

October 2015. You will learn to recognize and understand

different kinds of abuse … and learn how to come to grips

with what is happening in your life.

Find out how to make it happen and turn it around!

J'Anmetra Waddell, a motivational speaker, is available for workshops and speaking engagements.

To book J'Anmetra for *your* event (small groups are welcome), contact her via one of the avenues listed below:

Email: **Janmetra@waddellconsult.com**
Web: **www.WaddellConsult.com**
Phone: 4045908174
Twitter: Janmetra

28886703R00057

Made in the USA
Columbia, SC
18 October 2018